The Best of Sacred Music

Piano/Vocal Sheet Music Arrangements

Volume One
A thru L

THE
CREATIVE
CONCEPTS
LIBRARY
BOOK NINE

Catalog #07-1117

ISBN# 1-56922-180-4

©1998 CREATIVE CONCEPTS PUBLISHING CORPORATION
All Rights Reserved

Cover Painting by Mary Woodin - London, England

EXCLUSIVELY DISTRIBUTED BY
HAL•LEONARD® CORPORATION
7777 W. BLUEMOUND RD. P.O. BOX 13819 MILWAUKEE, WI 53213

Visit Hal Leonard Online at
www.halleonard.com

CONTENTS

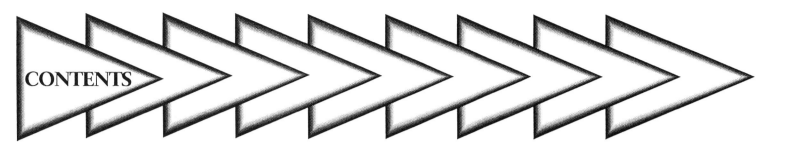

CONTENTS

Abide With Me

Words by Henry F. Lyte

Music by William H. Monk

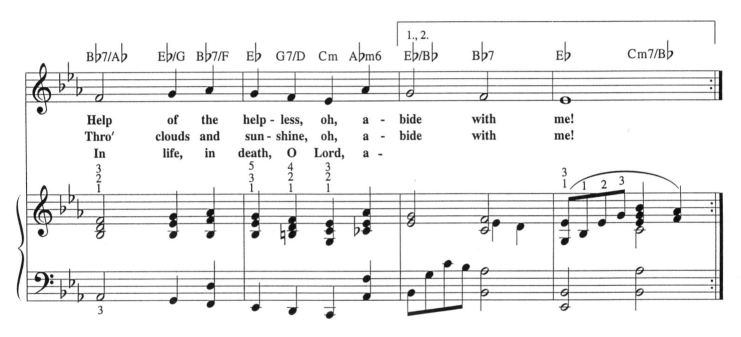

Abide With Me

All God's Children Got Shoes

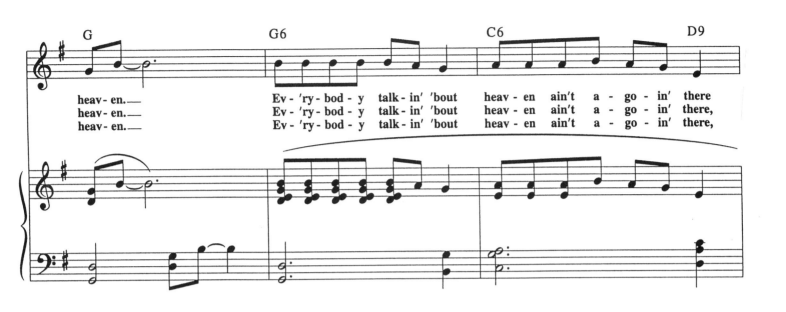

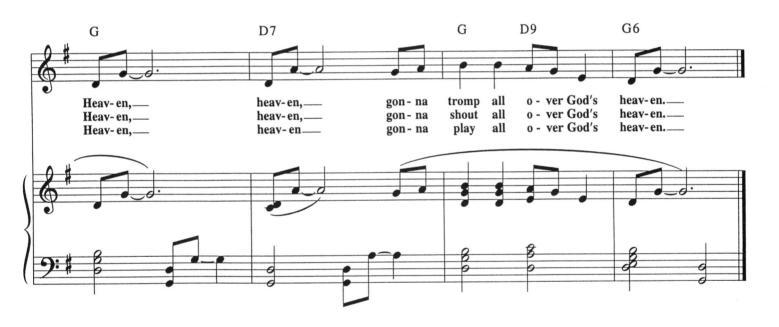

4.
I got a song, you got a song,
All God's children got songs.
When I get to heaven gonna sing my song,
Gonna sing all over God's heaven heaven, heaven
Ev'rybody talkin' 'bout heaven ain't a-goin' there,
Heaven, Heaven,
Gonna sing all over God's heaven

5.
I got wings, you got wings,
All God's children got wings.
When I get to heaven gonna put on my wings,
Gonna fly
All over God's heaven, heaven, heaven.
Ev'rybody talkin' 'bout heaven ain't a-goin' there,
Heaven, Heaven,
Gonna fly all over God's heaven

All Hail the Power of Jesus' Name

Words by Edward Perronet

Music by Oliver Holden

All Hail the Power of Jesus' Name

Amazing Grace

*Words by John Newton
and John P. Rees*

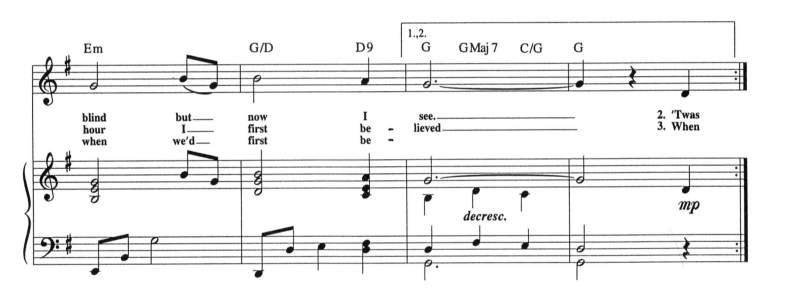

Ave Maria

By Franz Schubert

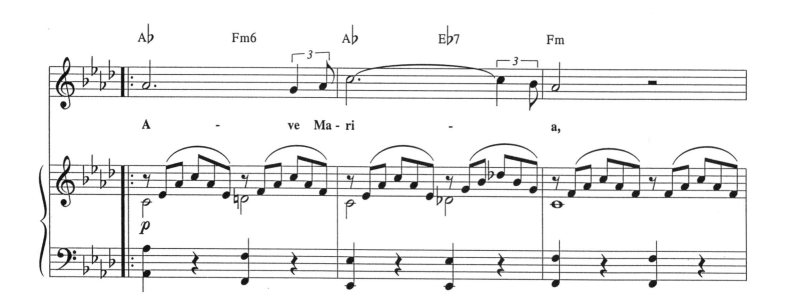

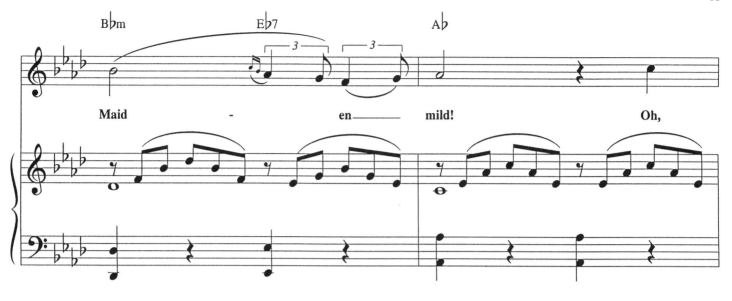

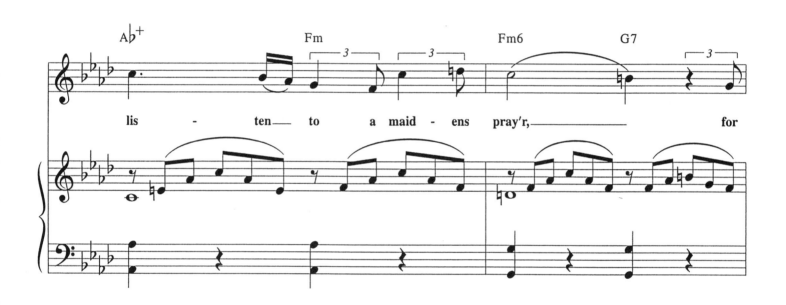

Ave Maria

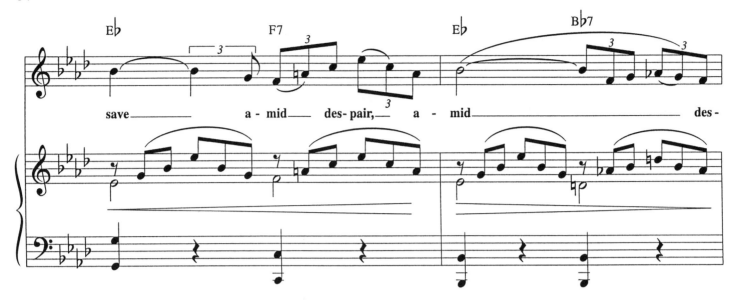

save _____ a - mid _____ des- pair, _____ a - mid _____ des -

pair. Safe may _____ we sleep be-neath Thy

care _____ Tho' ban - ished, out - cast and _____ re -

Ave Maria

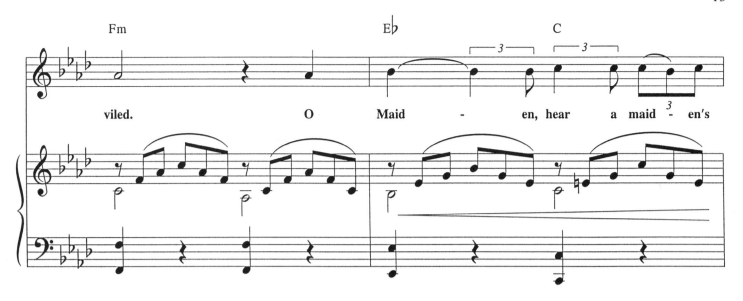

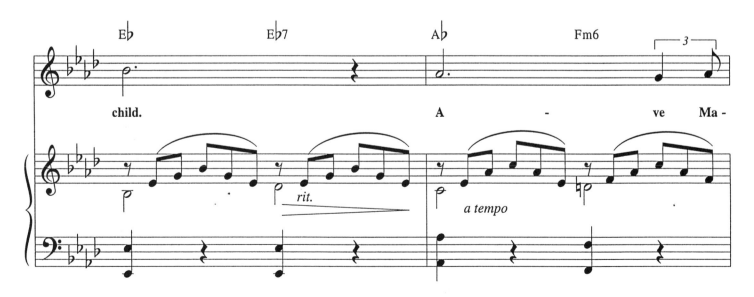

Ave Maria

ri - a!

Ave Maria

Battle Hymn of the Republic

Words by Julia Ward Howe

Music by William Steffe

Battle Hymn of the Republic

Battle Hymn of the Republic

Beautiful Isle of Somewhere

By John Fearis

1. Some-where the sun is shin - ing, Some-where the song-birds dwell,___
2. Some-where the day is long - er, Some-where the task in done,___

Hush, then, thy sad re - pin - ing, God lives, and all___ is well.___
Some-where the heart is strong - er, Some-where the guer - don won.___

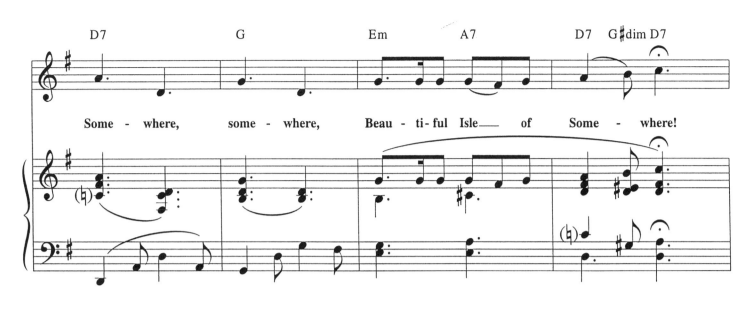

Some - where, some - where, Beau - ti - ful Isle— of Some - where!

Land of the true, where we live a - new, Beau - ti - ful Isle— of Some - where.

Some - where the load is lift - ed Close by an o - pen gate,—

Beautiful Isle of Somewhere

Beautiful Isle of Somewhere

Be Still, My Soul

Words by Katharina von Schlegel

Music by Jean Sibelius

1. Be still, my soul, the Lord is on thy side;
2. Be still, my soul, thy God doth un - der - take
3. Be still, my soul, the hour is has - tening on

Bear pa - tient - ly the cross of grief or pain.
To guide the fu - ture as He has the past.
When we shall be for - ev - er with the Lord.

24

Be Still My Soul

Be Still My Soul

Blessed Assurance

Words by Fanny J. Crosby
Music by Phoebe P. Knapp

Blessed Redeemer

By Avis B. Christiansen
and Harry Dixon Loes

29

Blessed Redeemer

Blessed Redeemer

Day by Day

Words by Carolina Sandell-Berg

Music by Oscar Ahnfelt

Day By Day

Day By Day

Blest Be the Tie That Binds

Words by John Fawcett

Music by Johann G. Näegeli

Blest Be the Tie That Binds

Brighten the Corner
Where You Are

Words by Ina Duley Ogden
Music by Charles H. Gabriel

By an' By

The Church's One Foundation

Words by Samuel J. Stone

Music by Samuel S. Wesley

With motion

The Church's One Foundation

Come, Thou Almighty King

By Felice de Giardini

Come, Thou Almighty King

Christ the Lord Is Risen Today

Words by Charles Wesley

Music from Lyra Davidica

With Motion

1. Christ the Lord is ris'n to - day,— Al - le - lu - ia!
2. Lives a - gain our glo - rious King,— Al - le - lu - ia!
3. Soar we now where Christ has led,— Al - le - lu - ia!

Sons of men and an - gels say:— Al - le - lu - ia!
Where, O death, is now thy sting?— Al - le - lu - ia!
Fol - l'wing our ex - alt - ed Head,— Al - le - lu - ia!

Christ the Lord Is Risen Today

Deep River

Do, Lord

Doxology (Praise God)

Down by the Riverside

An Evening Prayer

Words & Music by
C.M. Battersby and
Charles H. Gabriel

Ev'ry Time I Feel the Spirit

Ezekiel Saw The Wheel

4. There's one thing sure that you can't do, 'way in the middle of the air,
   You can't serve God and Satan, too, 'way in the middle of the air.

   Chorus

5. One of these days about twelve o'clock, 'way in the middle of the air,
   This old world's gonna reel and rock, 'way in the middle of the air.

   Chorus

Fairest Lord Jesus

Fairest Lord Jesus

Faith of Our Fathers

Words by Frederick W. Faber

Music by Henry F. Hemy

Faith of Our Fathers

Faith of Our Fathers

Kum Ba Yah

4. Someone's hoping, Lord, kum ba yah,
   Someone's hoping, Lord, kum ba yah!
   Someone's hoping, Lord, kum ba yah,
   O Lord, kum ba yah.

5. Someone's dancing, Lord, kum ba yah,
   Someone's dancing, Lord, kum ba yah!
   Someone's dancing, Lord, kum ba yah,
   O Lord, kum ba yah.

6. Someone's shouting, Lord, kum ba yah,
   Someone's shouting, Lord, kum ba yah!
   Someone's shouting, Lord, kum ba yah,
   O Lord, kum ba yah.

7. Someone's praying, Lord, kum ba yah,
   Someone's praying, Lord, kum ba yah!
   Someone's praying, Lord, kum ba yah,
   O Lord, kum ba yah.

Give Me That Old Time Religion

God of Our Fathers

Words by Daniel C. Roberts

Music by George W. Warren

God of Our Fathers

God Will Take Care of You

Words by Civilla D. Martin

Music by W. Stillman Martin

1. Be not dis- mayed— what - e'er be - tide, God will take care of you.——
2. All you may need— He will pro- vide, God will take care of you.——
3. No mat- ter what— may be the test, God will take care of you.——

Be - neath His wings— of love a - bide, God will take care of you.
Noth - ing you ask— will be de - nied, God will take care of you.
Lean, wea - ry one,— up - on His breast, God will take care of you.

God Will Take Care of You

Go Down, Moses

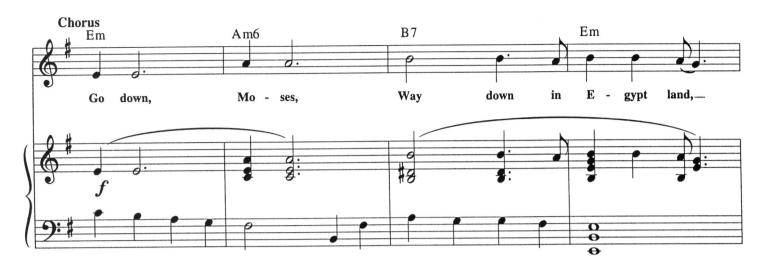

4.
Tle Lord told Moses what to do
Let my people go,
To lead the Hebrew children through
Let my people go.
Chorus

5.
O come along Moses, you won't get lost
Let my people go,
Stretch out your rod and come across,
Let my people go.
Chorus

6.
As Israel stood by the waterside,
Let my people go,
At God's command it did divide,
Let my people go.
Chorus

7.
When they reached the other shore
Let my people go,
They sang a song of triumph o'er,
Let my people go.
Chorus

8.
Pharoah said he'd go across,
Let my people go,
But Pharoah and his host were lost,
Let my people go.
Chorus

9.
Jordan shall stand up like a wall,
Let my people go,
And the walls of Jericho shall fall,
Let my people go.
Chorus

10.
Your foes shall not before you stand,
Let my people go,
And you'll possess fair Canaan's Land
Let my people go.
Chorus

11.
We need not always weep and mourn,
Let my people go,
And wear these slavery chains forlorn,
Let my people go.
Chorus

Good News

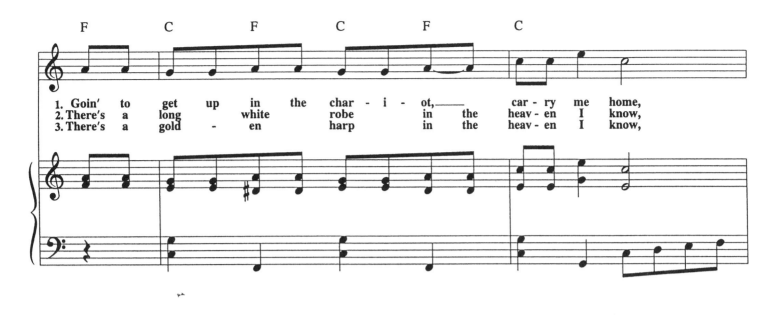

1. Goin' to get up in the char - i - ot,___ car - ry me home,
2. There's a long white robe in the heav - en I know,
3. There's a gold - en harp in the heav - en I know,

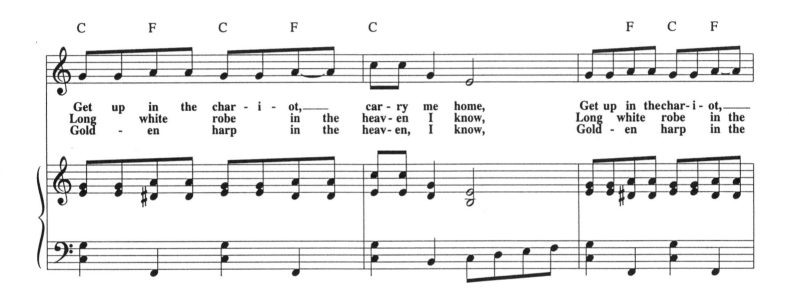

Get up in the char - i - ot,___ car - ry me home, Get up in the char - i - ot,___
Long white robe in the heav - en I know, Long white robe in the
Gold - en harp in the heav - en, I know, Gold - en harp in the

D.C. al Fine

car - ry me home,
heav - en I know, An' I don't want her leave - a me be - hind.
heav - en I know,

Great Day

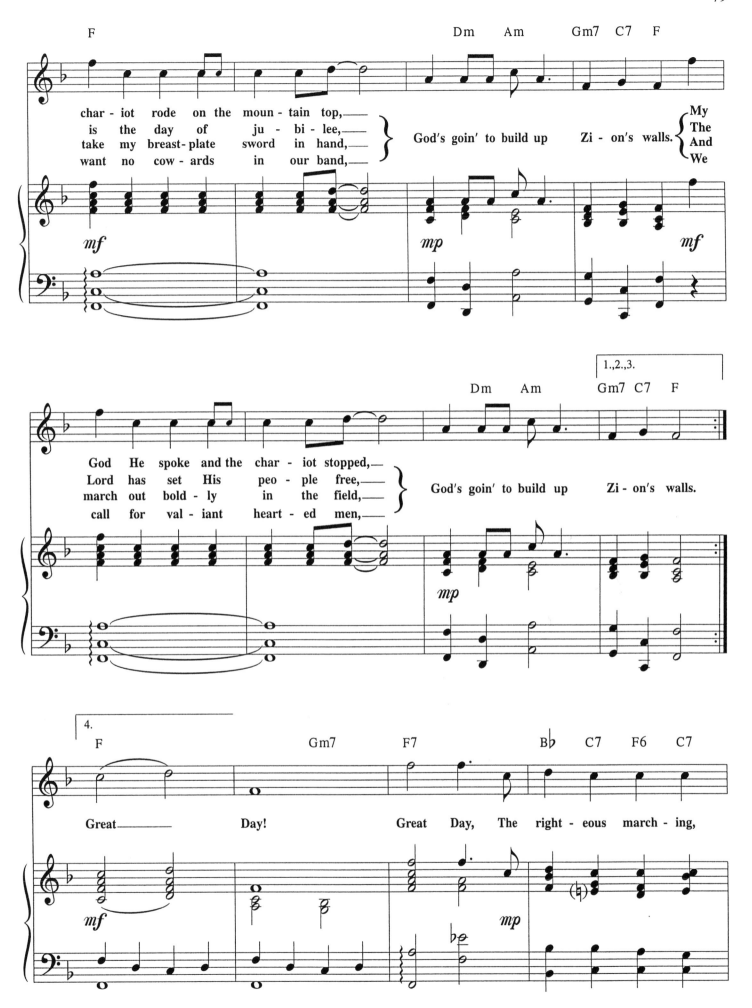

Great Day

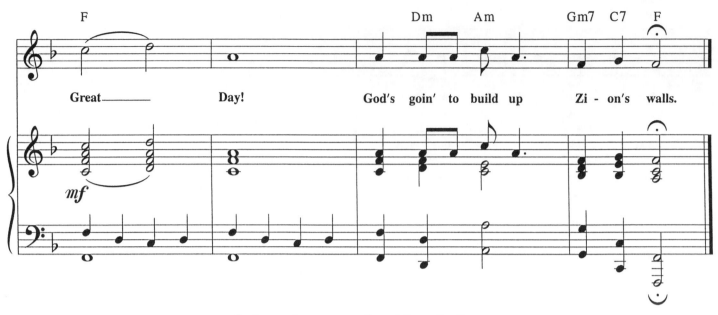

Great_____ Day! God's goin' to build up Zi - on's walls.

He Leadeth Me

Words by Joseph Gilmore

Music by William B. Bradbury

Moderately

1. He

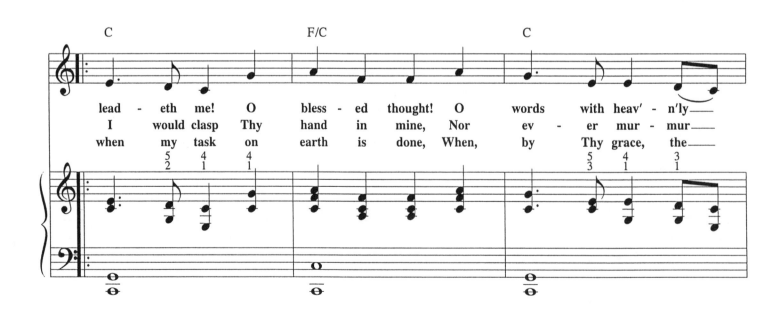

lead - eth me! O bless - ed thought! O words with heav' - n'ly_____
I would clasp Thy hand in mine, Nor ev - er mur - mur_____
when my task on earth is done, When, by Thy grace, the_____

He Leadeth Me

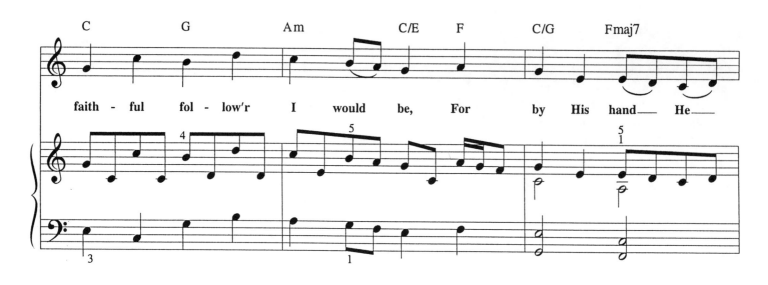

faith - ful fol - low'r I would be, For by His hand___ He___

lead - eth me.

2. Lord,
3. And lead - eth me.

He Leadeth Me

His Eye Is on the Sparrow

Words by Civilla D. Martin

Music by Charles H. Gabriel

His Eye Is on the Sparrow

His Eye Is on the Sparrow

Here Comes Jesus

Traditional

1. Here Comes Je - sus,_____ see Him walk - ing on the wa - ter,
2. Here Comes Je - sus,_____ see Him feed five thou - sand peo - ple,

He'll lift you up,_____ and he'll help_____ you stand;_____
He lift - ed them up,_____ and He helped them to stand;_____

Here Comes Jesus

He's Got The Whole World
In His Hands

Holy, Holy, Holy

Words by Reginald Heber

Music by John B. Dykes

Holy, Holy, Holy

Hush! Hush!

I Love To Tell the Story

Words and Music by
Katherine Hankey and William G. Fischer

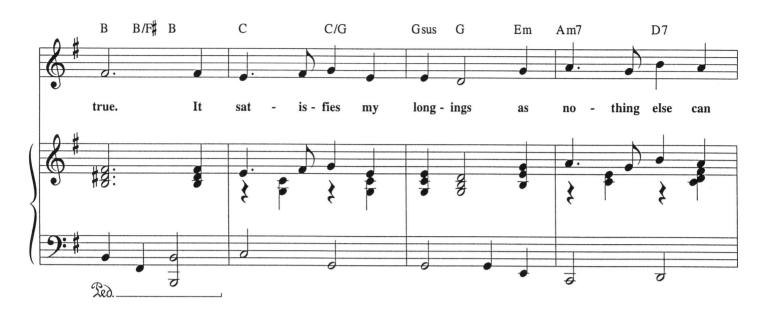

true. It sat - is - fies my long - ings as no - thing else can

do. I love to tell the sto - ry, 'Twill be my theme in

glo - ry to tell the old,— old sto - ry of Je - sus and His love.

I Love To Tell the Story

I Need Thee Every Hour

Words by Annie S. Hawks
and Robert Lowry
Music by Robert Lowry

I Surrender All

Words by Judson W. Van DeVenter

Music by Winfield S. Weeden

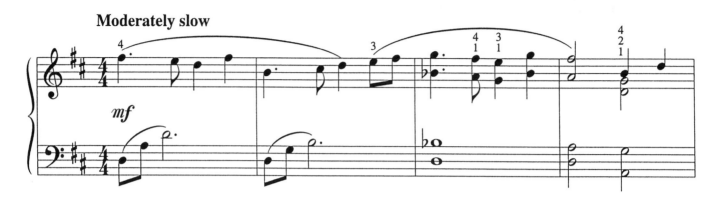

1. All to Je-sus I sur-ren-der, All to Him I free-ly give.
2. All to Je-sus I sur-ren-der, Hum-bly at His feet I bow.
3. All to Je-sus I sur-ren-der, Lord, I give my-self to Thee.

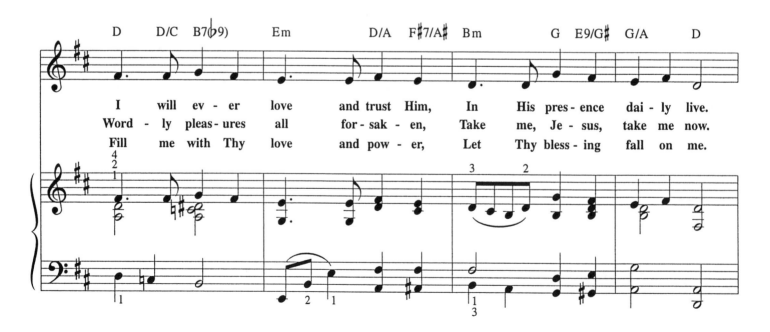

I will ev-er love and trust Him, In His pres-ence dai-ly live.
Word-ly pleas-ures all for-sak-en, Take me, Je-sus, take me now.
Fill me with Thy love and pow-er, Let Thy bless-ing fall on me.

I Surrender All

I Would Be Like Jesus

Words and Music by
B. D. Ackley and James Rowe

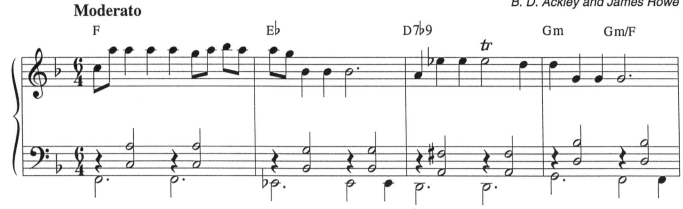

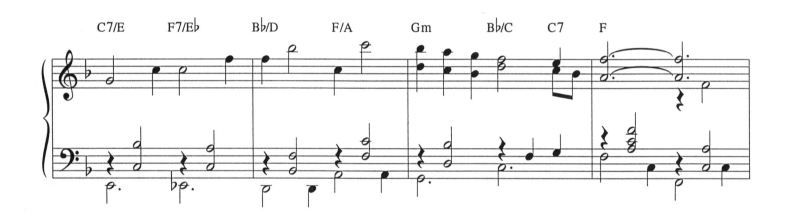

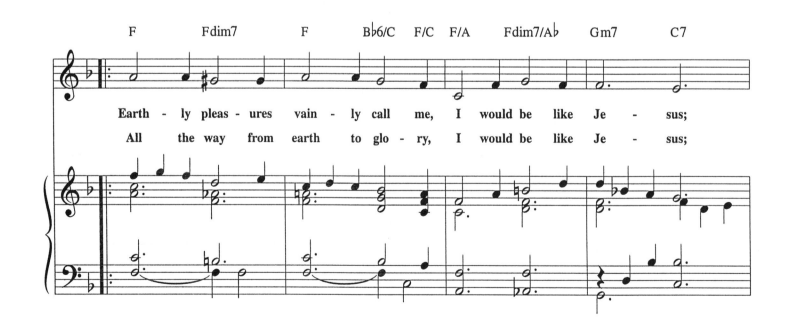

Earth - ly pleas - ures vain - ly call me, I would be like Je - sus;

All the way from earth to glo - ry, I would be like Je - sus;

I Would Be Like Jesus

Jesus Wants Me For A Sunbeam

Words by Nellie Talbot

Music by Edwin O. Excell

Jesus Wants Me For A Sunbeam

In the Garden

Words and Music by
C. Austin Miles

1.I come to the gar - den a - lone, While the
2. speaks, and the sound of His voice Is so
3. stay in the gar - den with Him Tho' the

dew is still on the ro - ses, And the voice I hear fall-ing
sweet the birds hush their sing - ing, And the mel - o - dy, That He
night a - rouns me be fall - ing, But He bids me go; Thro'the

on my ear The Son of God dis - clos - es.
gave to me With - in my heart is ring - ing.
voice of woe His voice to me is call - ing.

It Is Well With My Soul

Words by Horatio G. Spafford
Music by Philip P. Bliss

In the Sweet By and By

In the sweet by and by, we shall meet on that beau - ti - ful shore. In the sweet by and by we shall

meet on that beau - ti - ful shore. We shall shore.
To our

In the Sweet By and By

Ivory Palaces

By Henry Barraclough

Refrain

Out of the iv - o - ry pal - a - ces In - to a world of woe,

On - ly His great e - ter - nal love Made my Sav-ior go. 2. His 3. His

go. 4. In go.

Ivory Palaces

Jesus Loves Me

Words by Anna B. Warner
Music by William B. Bradbury

Joshua Fought the Battle of Jericho

Just A Closer Walk With Thee

Slowly, with a lilt

Just a clos - er walk with Thee.

Grant it, Je - sus, is my plea.

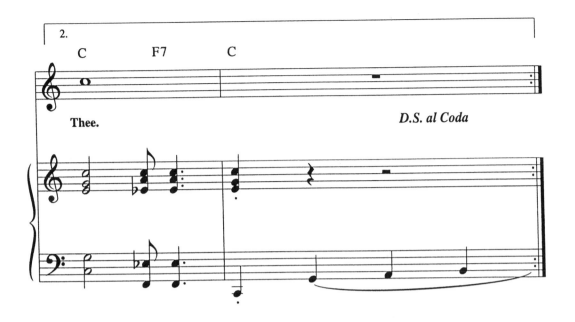

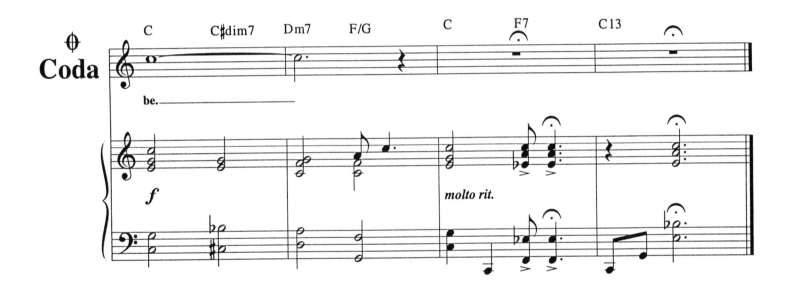

Just a Little Talk with Jesus

Just As I Am

Words by Charlotte Elliott
Music by William B. Bradbury

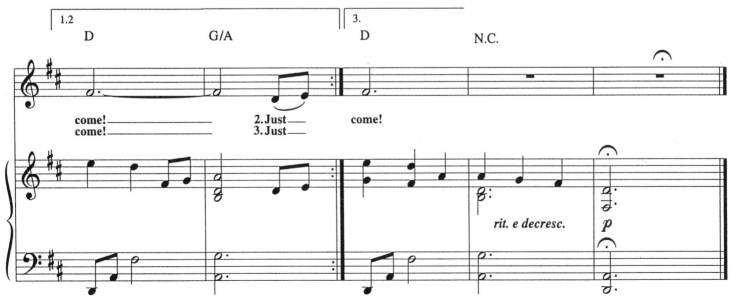

The Last Mile of the Way

By Johnson Oatman, Jr. and
Wm. Edie Marks

The Last Mile of the Way

Let Us Break Bread Together

Let Us Break Bread Together

Let Us Break Bread Together

The Lord Bless You and Keep You

By Peter C. Lutkin

Slowly, with expression

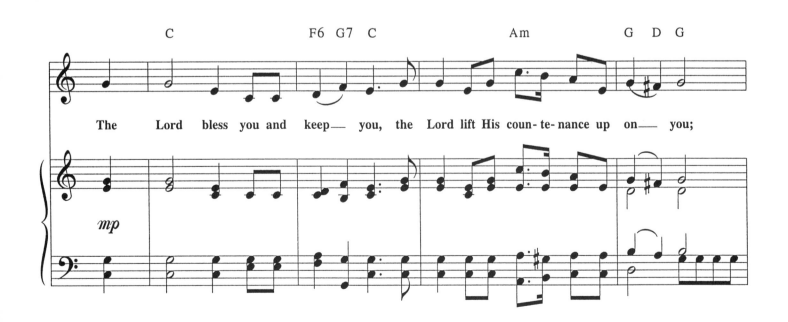

The Lord bless you and keep— you, the Lord lift His coun-te-nance up on— you;

The Lord Bless You And Keep You

The Lord Bless You and Keep You

The Lord Is My Shepherd

By W. S. Passmore
and Henry Smart

The Lord Is My Shepherd

The Lord Is My Shepherd

The Lord Is My Shepherd

The Lord's Prayer

by Felix Mendelssohn

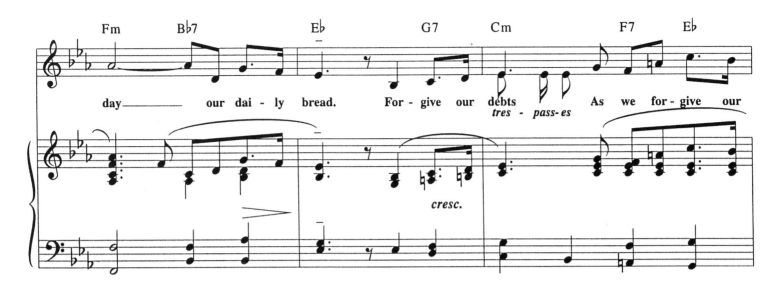

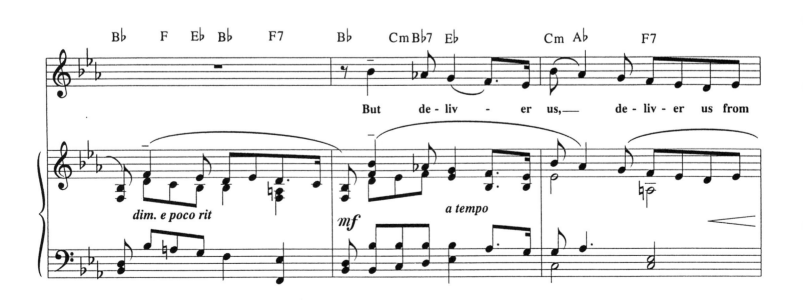

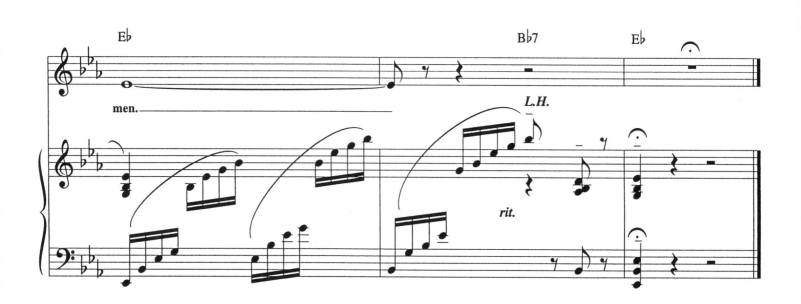

How Great Thou Art

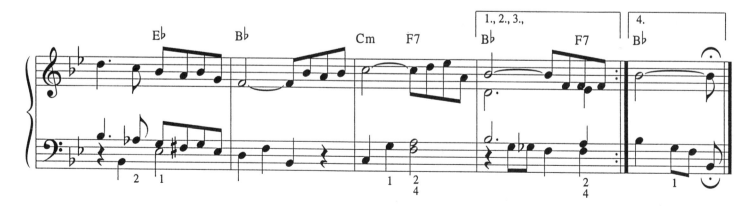

The Lost Chord

Words by Adelaide A Proctor

Music by Arthur Sullivan

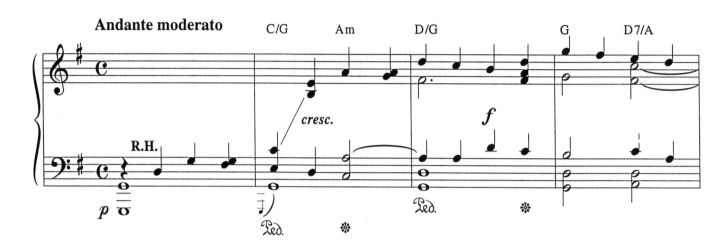

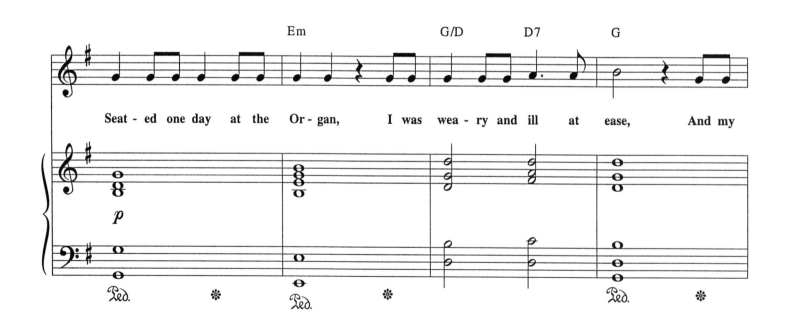

Seat - ed one day at the Or - gan, I was wea - ry and ill at ease, And my

The Lost Chord

144

The Lost Chord

The Lost Chord

The Lost Chord

The Lost Chord

The Lost Chord

Love Lifted Me

Words by James Rowe
Music by Howard E. Smith

Verse:

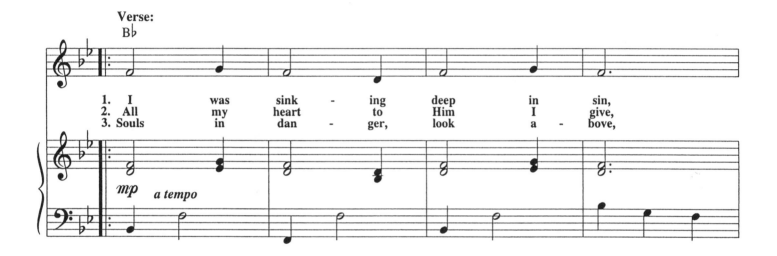

1. I was sink - ing deep in sin,
2. All my heart to Him I give,
3. Souls in dan - ger, look a - bove,

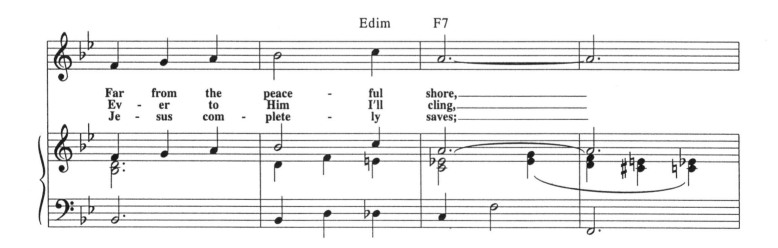

Far from the peace - ful shore,
Ev - er to Him I'll cling,
Je - sus com - plete - ly saves;

The Love of God

Words and Music by F. M. Lehman

The Love Of God

The Love Of God